ULTIMATE CAR BATTLES

MUSTANG vs. CORVETTE

Colin Crum

WINDMILL
BOOKS

New York

Published in 2014 by Windmill Books, An Imprint of Rosen Publishing
29 East 21st Street, New York, NY 10010

First Edition

Produced for Windmill by Cyan Candy, LLC
Designer: Erica Clendening, Cyan Candy
Editor for Windmill: Joshua Shadowens

Photo Credits: Cover (top), pp. 4, 8, 24, 26, 30 (bottom) Darren Brode/Shutterstock.com; cover (bottom), p. 23 Chris Curtis/Shutterstock.com; p. 5 dutourdumonde/Shutterstock.com; p. 6 © BrokenSphere / Wikimedia Commons; p. 7 CJ DUB, via Wikimedia Commons; p. 9 tratong/Shutterstock.com; p. 10 Wichan Kongchan/Shutterstock.com; pp. 11, 12 Radoslaw Lecyk/Shutterstock.com; p. 13 Gary Whitton/Shutterstock.com; p. 14 DeepGreen/Shutterstock.com; p. 15 littleny/Shutterstock.com; p. 16 Alexander Snahovskyy/Shutterstock.com; p. 17 350z33 at en.wikipedia, via Wikimedia Commons; p. 18 Thor Jorgen Udvang / Shutterstock.com; p. 19 Michael Stokes / Shutterstock.com; p. 20 Bocman1973/Shutterstock.com; p. 21 http://www.flickr.com/people/33502302@N00 via Wikimedia Commons; p. 22 Paul Stringer / Shutterstock.com; p. 25 GTS Production/Shutterstock.com; p. 27 Zoran Karapancev/Shutterstock.com; p. 30 (top) Dongliu/Shutterstock.com

Library of Congress Cataloging-in-Publication Data

Crum, Colin.
 Mustang vs. Corvette / by Colin Crum. — First edition.
     pages cm. — (Ultimate car battles)
 Includes index.
 ISBN 978-1-4777-9007-6 (library) — ISBN 978-1-4777-9008-3 (pbk.) —
 ISBN 978-1-4777-9009-0 (6-pack)
 1. Mustang automobile—Juvenile literature. 2. Corvette automobile—Juvenile literature.
 I. Title. II. Title: Mustang versus Corvette.
 TL215.M8C78 2014
 629.222'2—dc23
                              2013021163

Manufactured in the United States of America

CPSIA Compliance Information: Batch #BW14WM: For Further Information contact Windmill Books, New York, New York at 1-866-478-0556

TWO FAN FAVORITES

In the battle for the all-time best American sports car, the Ford Mustang and the Chevrolet Corvette both put up a good fight! Although these famous cars are both fan favorites, they have very different styles. The Corvette is a classic American two-seater sports car. It is known for being beautiful and fast. The Mustang was America's first popular "pony car," meaning it is a smaller sporty car with

The 2011 Ford Mustang GT California Special is known for its fade black side stripes and side scoops. It also has a 32-valve, 5.0-liter V8 engine that can produce 412 horsepower!

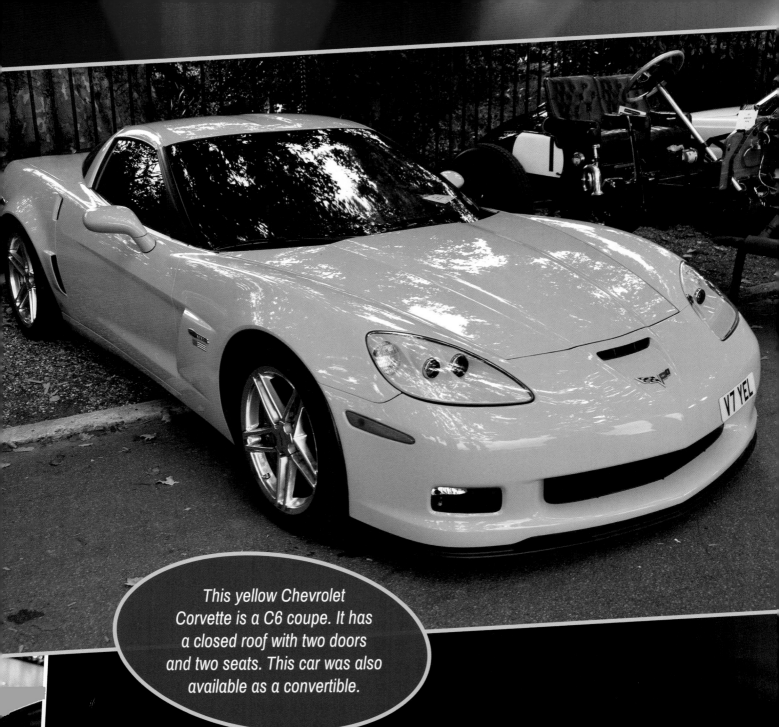

This yellow Chevrolet Corvette is a C6 coupe. It has a closed roof with two doors and two seats. This car was also available as a convertible.

a powerful engine. In fact, the "pony car" design is actually named for the Ford Mustang!

The Mustang and the Corvette have both been made and sold continuously for decades. This means that, although they have been redesigned many times, these cars have not stopped being produced since they were first made. Both cars have also won the Motor Trend Car of the Year award twice!

WHAT MAKES A MUSTANG?

The Ford Mustang is known for being stylish, sporty, and affordable. It is also known for its galloping horse **emblem**. This emblem was chosen for the mustang horse, which shares a name with the car.

Mustang horses are free-roaming horses once found all over the American West. The galloping Mustang emblem can be seen on the grille of many Mustang models. The Mustang's horse emblem is

Boss 429

The 1969 Boss 429 was a **high-performance** Mustang **variation** known for its large engine. In fact, Ford hired special designers to **modify** the 428 Cobra Jet and the Super Cobra Jet Mach 1 Mustang bodies so the Boss 429 engine would fit! Today, this car is considered very rare. Less than 1,400 Boss 429s were made between 1969 and 1970.

This is a 1968 Shelby GT 500-KR convertible. KR stands for King of the Road! This Mustang was powered by a newly-designed 7.0-liter Cobra Jet GT V8 engine.

also the reason its design was nicknamed a "pony car." Mustang fans like to argue about which Mustang is the all-time best. Some favorites are the 1968 Mustang Shelby GT 500-KR, the 1978 Mustang II King Cobra, and the 1986 Mustang SVO!

ALL ABOUT CORVETTES

The Chevrolet Corvette is one of most popular American sports cars of all time. It has been around for more than 60 years. 'Vettes can be seen on roads, tracks, and at car shows around the world! They are known for being sleek and speedy. Every Corvette fan has their favorite model year or special edition car!

Although it has always been beautiful, the Corvette has come a long way in **engineering** and performance over the years. For example, Corvette's first model only had a two-speed transmission. However, the 2014 Corvette Stingray has a seven-speed Tremec TR6070 manual transmission!

This is the 2014 Corvette C7 Stingray, shown at the Chicago Auto Show in February 2013. Visitors to the show were impressed by the Stingray's **aerodynamic** curves!

Restored 427 Corvette Convertible

35th Anniversary Corvette

In 1988, Chevrolet offered a special edition 'Vette to celebrate Corvette's 35th Anniversary. This "Triple White Corvette" was a white coupe with white wheels and a white interior, including a white steering wheel. Each car had a special numbered plaque on the console. Just 2,050 were built!

MUSTANG'S BEGINNINGS

In the early 1960s, the Ford Motor Company had an idea to make a sleek, speedy sports car like popular European models. However, Ford wanted its car to be affordable, and to be able to fit four people instead of two.

This made more sense for American families than an expensive two-seater sports car! With this in mind, they designed the Mustang.

In order to make the Mustang affordable, Ford used many parts from another

A 1st-generation Mustang

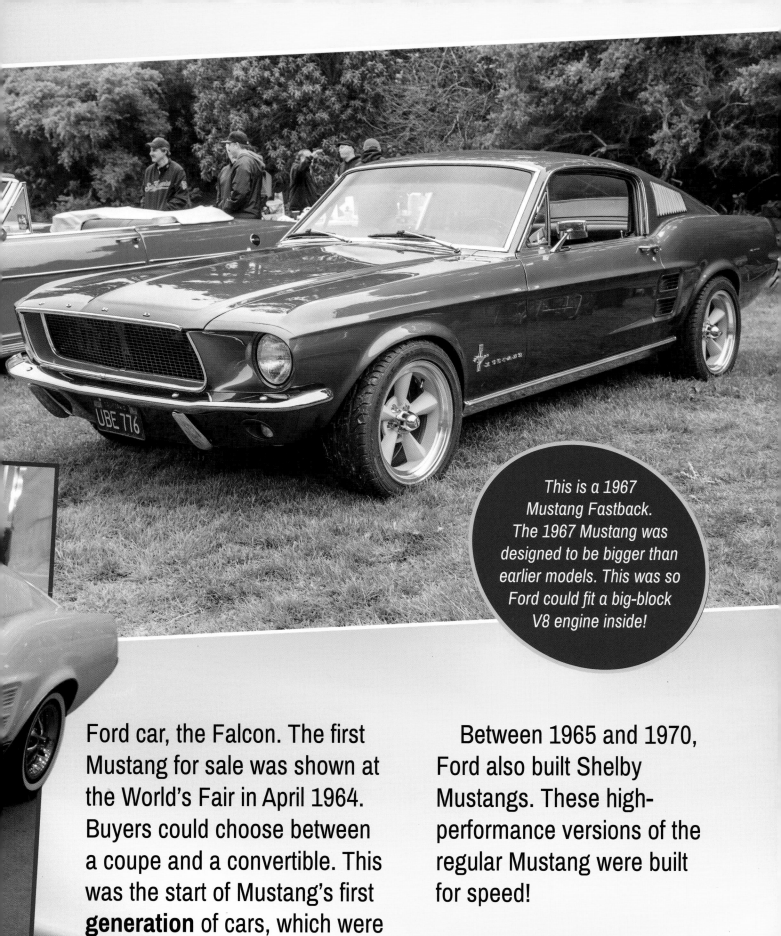

This is a 1967 Mustang Fastback. The 1967 Mustang was designed to be bigger than earlier models. This was so Ford could fit a big-block V8 engine inside!

Ford car, the Falcon. The first Mustang for sale was shown at the World's Fair in April 1964. Buyers could choose between a coupe and a convertible. This was the start of Mustang's first **generation** of cars, which were sold until 1973.

Between 1965 and 1970, Ford also built Shelby Mustangs. These high-performance versions of the regular Mustang were built for speed!

THE START OF CORVETTE

In the 1950s, Americans fell in love with cool British sports cars. However, General Motors did not make any cars like the British cars Americans wanted to buy! GM's head designer decided to make a **concept car** based on his ideas for a smooth, beautiful sports car. After seeing the concept car, Chevrolet's head engineer decided to put it into production. This became the first generation, or C1, Corvette!

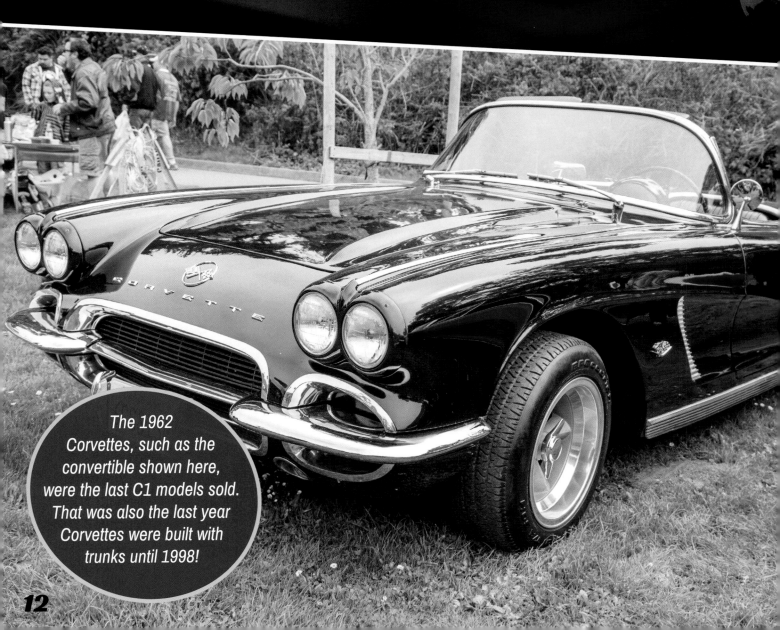

The 1962 Corvettes, such as the convertible shown here, were the last C1 models sold. That was also the last year Corvettes were built with trunks until 1998!

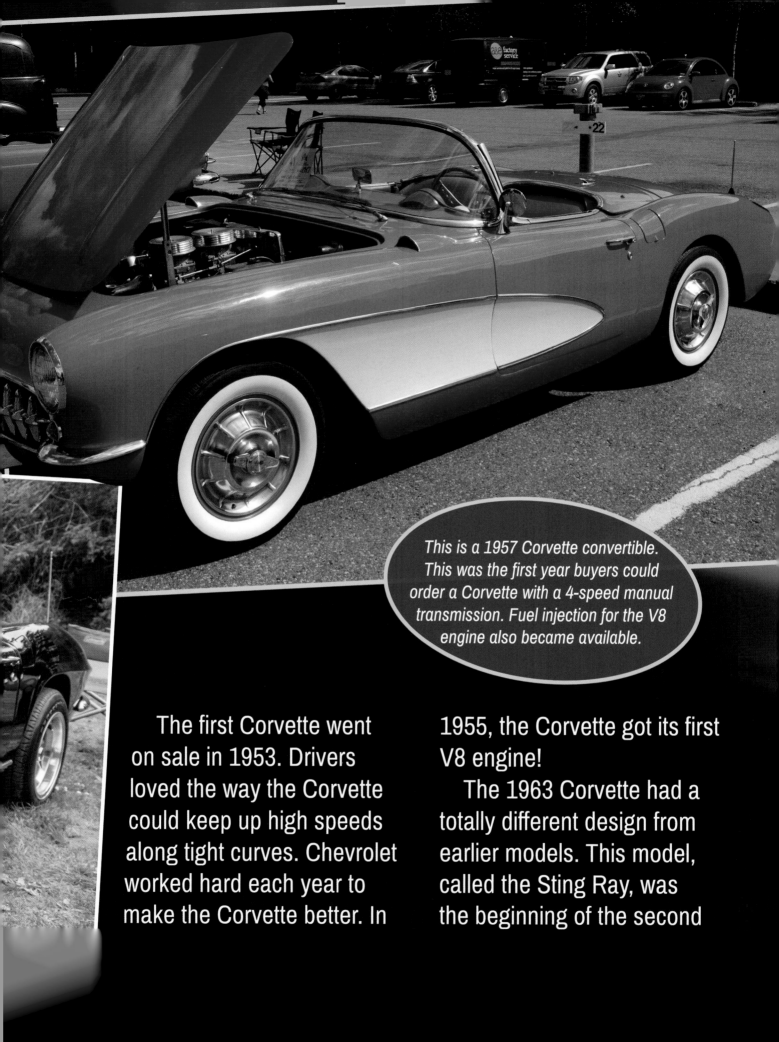

This is a 1957 Corvette convertible. This was the first year buyers could order a Corvette with a 4-speed manual transmission. Fuel injection for the V8 engine also became available.

The first Corvette went on sale in 1953. Drivers loved the way the Corvette could keep up high speeds along tight curves. Chevrolet worked hard each year to make the Corvette better. In 1955, the Corvette got its first V8 engine!

The 1963 Corvette had a totally different design from earlier models. This model, called the Sting Ray, was the beginning of the second

MUSTANGS OVER TIME

Mustangs have gone through many changes over the years. The Mustang II was sold between 1974 and 1978. The 1974 model was smaller and less powerful because the United States was going through an oil crisis. However, engine performance got better with the 1976 Cobra II and 1978 King Cobra designs.

Third-generation Mustangs were made between 1979 and 1993. They had a boxy design that did not look like the original Mustang. Some had

1971 Mustang Mach 1

LB 600 BY

These Ford Mustangs are on display at an auto show in Long Island, New York. An auto show is a good place to see different generations of Mustang models!

four headlights, and later models had no grilles!

From 1994 to 2004, Ford offered a redesigned fourth-generation Mustang with Ford's "New Edge" style. These Mustangs were designed with sharp contours and creases, and large wheel arches.

2001 Mustang Bullitt

In 2001, Ford built a special version of the Mustang GT called the Mustang Bullitt. The Bullitt was named after a 1968 movie featuring actor Steve McQueen. In the movie, McQueen drives a dark green Mustang GT 390 Fastback in a famous high-speed chase. Fans liked this car because it reminded them of the classic Mustang!

CHANGING CORVETTES

Over the years, many changes have been made to the way Corvettes look. However, their performance keeps getting better and better!

C3 Corvettes were sold between 1968 and 1982. Chevrolet celebrated Corvette's 25th anniversary in 1978! A newly redesigned C4 Corvette was built in 1983. In 1986, Chevrolet sold the first Corvette convertibles since 1975.

Chevrolet introduced the C5 Corvette in 1997. This model had a curvy style and

The 2009 50th Anniversary Corvette Stingray was a special concept car displayed at auto shows. This car also appeared in the 2009 movie Transformers: Revenge of the Fallen.

This white Corvette Sting Ray convertible was driven by astronaut Alan Shepard. Alan Shepard was a big fan of Corvettes. He was also the first American to travel in space!

could reach a top speed of 181 miles per hour (291 km/h)! The C6 Corvette was launched in 2005 with a 6-liter V8 engine that was replaced with a 7-liter V8 in 2006. The last C6 Corvette was built in 2013.

1969 AstroVette

In 1969, Chevrolet offered astronauts from NASA's space programs Corvettes to drive for one year. These Corvettes were called AstroVettes. The most famous AstroVettes belonged to three astronauts from the Apollo 12 space mission, Alan Bean, Richard Gordon, and Charles "Pete" Conrad Jr. Their AstroVettes were matching gold and black Corvette Stingray coupes!

MUSTANGS IN RACING

Mustangs can be seen speeding along in track, road, and drag races! Mustang first built GT-350s for Sports Car Club of America (SCCA) racing in 1965. In 1969, some of Mustang's most famous racing cars ever, the 428 Mach 1, Boss 429, and Boss 302, set speed records at the Bonneville Salt Flats in Utah.

Since the 1960s, Mustang has continued to race and win titles in SCCA races. They have

This Ford Mustang GT3 racecar was built by the Marc VDS Racing Team from Belgium. It is shown racing in the 2012 Dunlop 24 Hours Race at the Dubai Autodrome.

Here you can see a Mustang that has been given many modifications for drag racing. This car took part in the 2010 Easter Thunderball Drag Race in Northamptonshire, England.

also taken part in International Motor Sports Association (IMSA) GTO class racing since the 1980s. In 2005, 2008, and 2009, Mustang FR500C and GT models helped win Grand-Am Road Racing Continental Tire Sports Car Challenge championships for Ford.

In 2011, Mustang became Ford's stock car for NASCAR's Nationwide Series. Mustangs may also be racing in NASCAR's Spring Cup by 2014!

CORVETTES IN RACING

Corvette is famous in racing as a pace car for the Indianapolis 500 race. A Corvette has served as the pace car for this race 12 times between 1978 and 2013! Although pace cars do not compete in the race, they must be very fast on the track. Pace cars lead the racing cars in a warm-up lap in order to set the pace, or speed, for the start of the race. Pace cars also act as safety cars. When there

Corvette C3

Here, a Corvette C6.R racecar is driven by the Larbre Competition team in the 2011 24 Hours of Le Mans. This car finished the race first in its class!

is something blocking the track, the pace car enters the race ahead of the leading car. Then, it signals the other cars to slow down or stop.

Pratt & Miller's Corvette Racing team also drives special racing Corvettes in GT races. The Corvette C5-R and C6.R both have won many races, including the 24 Hours of Daytona, 12 Hours of Sebring, and 24 Hours of Le Mans.

HEAD-TO-HEAD RACING

Mustangs and Corvettes are considered different classes of cars. Because of this, they do not have a long racing history against each other in motorsports. However, sports car fans love to argue about which car would win in a head-to-head race!

If you want to see a Mustang race a Corvette, one place you might see these two

A Mustang modified for drag racing

FM55 LPA

A Corvette C6
with racing stripes

cars speed head-to-head is a drag race. In a drag race, two cars race across a short distance to a finish line. Many motor speedways have quarter-mile-(0.4 km) long tracks for drag racing. There, many different model years and editions of Corvettes and Mustangs can race against each other!

Safety First!

Drag racing on a track should not be confused with street racing. Street racing on public roads is dangerous and illegal! Drag racing has many rules in place to keep drivers and fans safe. The National Hot Road Association is one group that sets rules and hosts drag racing events across the United States.

FIFTH-GENERATION MUSTANGS

The fifth-generation Mustang was first introduced in 2005. These Mustangs are built from Ford's D2C **platform**, which is a rear-wheel drive 2-door coupe.

The 2014 Mustang comes in ten different models. The V6 series models are the V6, the V6 Premium, and the V6 Convertible. They are each built with a V6 engine that produces 305 horsepower, or HP. The GT series models are the GT premium, GT Convertible, and GT Premium

This is the 2013 Boss 302 Laguna Seca Edition. Here, the car is displayed for visitors at the North American International Auto on January 11, 2012 in Detroit, Michigan.

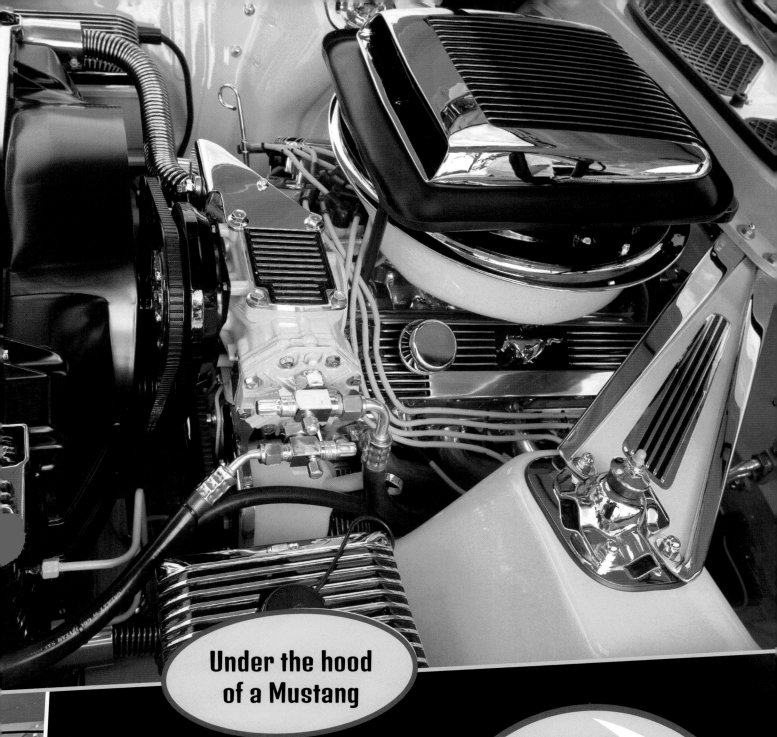

Under the hood of a Mustang

Convertible. These models have a more powerful 5-liter V8 engine that produces 420 HP. The Shelby GT500 and GT500 Convertible have 5.8-liter supercharged V8 engines that produce 662 HP!

Boss 302 Laguna Seca Edition

*The Boss 302 Laguna Seca edition is a limited edition version of Mustang's high-performance Boss 302. First sold in 1969 and 1970, Mustang created a two-year limited-run redesign of the Boss 302 for 2012 and 2013. The Laguna Seca edition was made for high-speed track use. Its front-splitter and spoiler greatly increase the model's **downforce**.*

THE C7 CORVETTE

Chevrolet revealed the seventh generation, or C7, Corvette in January 2013. Corvette celebrated its 60th anniversary in 2013! This car, also called the Corvette Stingray, became available for the 2014 model year. Chevrolet used many **elements** from the Corvette Racing program on the Stingray's exterior, including a carbon-fiber hood and roof and many vents. The Z51

Here, the 2014 C7 Stingray is on display at the North American International Auto Show on January 15, 2013 in Detroit, Michigan. This car is built with an aluminum frame.

2014 C7 Stingray

Performance Package includes different gear ratios, bigger brakes, and 19-inch (48.3 cm) front and 20-inch (51 cm) rear wheels.

Inside the car is a newly-designed Gen 5 Corvette LT1 6.2-liter V8 small block engine. This engine produces 450 HP. The 2014 Stingray can go from 0–60 miles per hour (0–97 km/h) in under four seconds. This car was designed for high-performance driving!

Corvette ZR1 Centennial Edition

*Chevrolet was started in 1911 and had its 100th birthday in 2011. To celebrate, Chevrolet offered a limited edition 2012 Corvette ZR1 called the **Centennial** Edition. This limited edition model had a satin-black body with satin-black wheels and red brake calipers. This color design was called Carbon Flash Metallic.*

27

THEN AND NOW

The Ford Mustang and the Chevrolet Corvette have both come a long way since their first models! One way to see how far these

MUSTANG

First Model	Early 1965 Mustang
Engine	V8 engine
Horsepower	210 horsepower
Transmission	4-speed manual transmission
0–60 mph (0–97 km/h)	7.5 seconds
Base Price	$2,557 (Convertible)

Latest Model	2014 Mustang Shelby GT500
Engine	5.8-liter V8 engine
Horsepower	662 horsepower
Transmission	6-speed manual transmission
0–60 mph (0–97 km/h)	3.2 seconds
Base Price	$54,800 (Convertible)

two cars have come is to compare the car's first model with its newest model. In the chart below, you can compare old and new Mustangs and Corvettes!

CORVETTE

First Model	**1953 Corvette**
Engine	**6-cylinder engine**
Horsepower	**150 horsepower**
Transmission	**2-speed automatic transmission**
0–60 mph (0–97 km/h)	**115 seconds**
Base Price	**$3,490 (Convertible)**
Latest Model	**2014 Corvette Stingray**
Engine	**6.2-liter V8 engine**
Horsepower	**450 horsepower**
Transmission	**7-speed manual transmission**
0–60 mph (0–97 km/h)	**3.9 seconds (estimated)**
Base Price	**$56,000 (Convertible)**

YOU DECIDE!

If you are a fan of American sports cars, it can be hard to choose between the Mustang and the Corvette. These two cars generally are not considered **rivals** because they are different classes of cars. One is a pony car, while the other is a classic sports car.

However, both the Mustang and the Corvette are known for being beautiful and speedy!

In a battle for the best all-time American sports car, the Mustang and the Corvette both rise to the top of the list! Which do you like better?

2011 Corvette C6

2012 Mustang Boss 302

GLOSSARY

aerodynamic (er-oh-dy-NA-mik) Made to move through the air easily.

anniversary (a-nuh-VERS-ree) The date on which an event occurred in the past or its special observance.

centennial (sen-TEH-nee-ul) Having to do with a hundredth anniversary.

concept car (KON-sept KAR) A car to show new features and technology.

downforce (DOWN-fors) The force of air pushing downward on something.

elements (EH-luh-ments) One of the parts that something is made of.

emblem (EM-blum) A sign or figure that stands for something.

engineering (en-juh-NEER-ing) The work that uses scientific knowledge for practical things, such as designing machines.

generation (jeh-nuh-RAY-shun) Things made during the same period.

high-performance (HY per-FOR-ments) A car that is designed for speed.

modify (MAH-dih-fy) To change something.

platform (PLAT-form) The basic structure on which a vehicle is built.

rivals (RY-vulz) Two people or companies who try to get or to do the same thing as one another.

variation (ver-ee-AY-shun) A different way of doing something.

FURTHER READING

Bullard, Lisa. *Chevrolet Corvette*. Fast Cars. Mankato, MN: Capstone Press, 2008.

Poolos, J. *Wild About Muscle Cars*. Wild Rides. New York: PowerKids Press, 2007.

Portman, Michael. *Mustangs*. Wild Wheels. New York: Gareth Stevens Learning Library, 2011.